931909

Y   Kallen, Stuart A.
031.02   Amazing human feats.
KAL

WORLD RECORD LIBRARY

AMAZING HUMAN FEATS

Written by:
Stuart Kallen

Published by Abdo & Daughters, 6535 Cecilia Circle, Edina, Minnesota 55439.

Library bound edition distributed by Rockbottom Books, Pentagon Tower, P.O. Box 36036, Minneapolis, Minnesota 55435.

Library of Congress Number: 91-073052   ISBN: 1-56239-049-X

Cover illustrated by: Terry Boles
Inside Photos by:
    Bettmann News Photo: 7-8, 10, 12, 14, 31
    Freelance Photographers Guild: 17

Edited by: Rosemary Wallner

TABLE OF CONTENTS

THANK YOUR BIG BRAINS

We live in a time like no other. While our ancestors might have only owned a club and a fur coat, our world today is filled with an infinite variety of *things*. Life today consists of a series of unconscious decisions and complex choices that would confuse and defeat creatures less intelligent than ourselves. Every day, we deal with an amazing array of modern machinery that helps us through our busy lives. We have reached this astounding point in history thanks to our big brains.

Back about five million years ago (a short amount of time in Earth's history), the distant relatives to human beings had small brains, about 300 cubic centimeters in size. These ape-like creatures used their tiny brains to invent simple tools and weapons. Then around two million years ago, the primitive brain began to grow rapidly. The first human-like creatures had brains that measured 750 cubic centimeters. These people, whom we usually associate with "cavemen," became ever more clever and invented more complex tools. As the centuries passed, human brains kept getting larger and larger.

With the evolution of speech, the brain started growing even faster. About 500,000 years ago, the brain began another spurt in growth. By the time modern humans emerged, about 100,000 years ago, the brain had grown to 1,400 cubic centimeters — over four times its original size. No other organ of any animal in the history of life on Earth has ever grown so fast.

HUMAN ACHIEVEMENT

Even though modern humans have been around for 100,000 years, many of our most amazing accomplishments have happened within the last 150 years. In that short amount of time humans have walked to the ends of the earth and even flown to the moon. Our giant brains have figured out ways for our bodies to survive frozen temperatures, hurl over land at 65 miles an hour in quiet comfort, and fly through space at speeds reaching 24,000 miles an hour.

Some people don't accept the commonplace and continually push the boundaries. The bravest men and women of our age have broken almost all physical barriers and have advanced science and humanity. And they've even had a little fun.

They've Been Everywhere — Two men hold the record for being the most traveled people in history. Parke G. Thompson of Akron, Ohio, and Giorgio Ricatto from Turin, Italy, have visited all 170 countries in the world and 61 of the 62 territories. Neither of the men have been to Heard Island or McDonald Island in the southern Indian Ocean. Let's hope they go there soon.

It's Lonely at the Top — No person has ever been as far away from any other human beings as Alfred M. Worden, Module pilot on the US *Apollo 15* lunar mission. When Worden flew the lunar mission on July 30, 1971, the nearest human being was 2,233.2 miles away.

Pilot Alfred M. Worden relaxes during final space suit pressure check.

*The Kunst brothers passed through this town on their
15,000 mile hike around the world.*

And Boy, Do Their Feet Hurt — The first person to have "walked around the world" was Steve Kunst. Kunst left his home in Waseca, Minnesota, on June 20, 1970, and walked through America, Europe, Asia, and Australia. He started the walk with his brother John, but John was killed by bandits in Afghanistan. Another brother, Peter, replaced him. Four different mules accompanied the Kunst brothers on their walk, including one named "Willie Makeit." The longest walk ended on October 5, 1974.

Tomas Pererira from Argentina spent ten years, from 1968 to 1978, walking 29,825 miles around five continents. Steve Newman of Bethel, Ohio, spent four years walking 22,500 miles around the world. Between April 1, 1983, and April 1, 1987, Newman walked through 20 countries on five continents.

Canadian Rick Hansen, who was paralyzed from the waist down because of a motorcycle accident, wheeled his wheelchair over 25,901 miles, through four continents and 34 countries. The journey started in March 1985 and ended in May 1987.

Canadian Rick Hansen, pictured here on a round the world tour in a wheel-chair.

Sean Maguire walked from Livengood, Alaska, to Key West, Florida. The 7,327 mile journey took 307 days and ended on April 9, 1979. Englishman John Lees walked across the continental United States from the City Hall in Los Angeles, California, to the City Hall in New York City in 53 days, 12 hours, and 15 minutes. During the 1972 journey, Lees averaged over 53 miles a day.

Journey to the Center of the Earth — The deepest penetration into the ground ever made by humans is 11,749 feet, or over two miles. This was accomplished at Wester Deep Levels Mine in Carletonville, South Africa. Because of the intense heat at the Earth's center, the rock temperature at that depth is 131 degrees Fahrenheit.

Water, Water Everywhere — Poon Lim holds the record for the longest survival on a raft at sea. Lim's ship, Great Britain's *SS Ben Lomand* was torpedoed by a German submarine on November 23, 1942. Lim floated in the Atlantic Ocean, about 565 miles from the nearest land, for 133 days. When he was picked up by a Brazilian fishing boat on April 5, 1943, he was able to walk ashore. Lim now lives in New York City.

Pictured here is 25 year old Poon Lim who survived 133 days alone on a raft in the South Atlantic.

LOVE AND MARRIAGE

It Must Be Love — Eddie Levin and Delphine Crha set the record for the world's longest kiss on September 24, 1984. The couple kissed for 17 days 10.5 hours in Chicago, Illinois. They celebrated setting the record with, what else, a kiss.

Thousands of Women Kissed by a Whale — James Whale of Leeds, England, kissed 4,525 women in eight hours for a Yorkshire Telethon on May 30, 1988. During the fund-raiser, Whale averaged one woman kissed every 6.36 seconds.

This Guy's a Real Wolf — Some sultans of Middle East countries have over 100 wives. But the man who holds the record for the most separate marriages is Glynn Wolfe. A former Baptist minister who was born in 1908 in Blythe, California, Wolfe has been married 27 different times. Wolfe married his first wife in 1927. His latest wife is 20-year-old Daisy Delgado from the Philippine Islands. Wolfe's oldest wife was 38 years old. He thinks he has 41 children, but has lost count.

Pictured between statues of two of his 27 wives, Glynn Wolfe holds the record for the most separate marriages.

I Do, I Do, I Do, I Do, I Do, I Do... — Linda Lou Essex of Anderson, Indiana, has been married 21 times, giving her the women's record for the most marriages. Essex married 15 men between 1957 and 1988, an average of one marriage every two years. She divorced her last husband in 1988.

Barred From Further Marriage — It seems that Giovanni Vigliotto couldn't say "I don't." Using the false name Fred Jipp, among 50 other aliases, Vigliotto married 104 women in 27 states and 14 countries between 1949 and 1981. In 1968, he married four different women aboard one ship that was sailing to Europe. Vigliotto's marrying days came to an end in Phoenix, Arizona, on March 28, 1983, when he was sentenced to 34 years in prison and fined $336,000 for fraud and bigamy.

Where Did *They* Honeymoon? — The oldest people to "tie the knot" were Harry Stevens, 103, and Thelma Lucas, 84. The elder lovebirds were married on December 3, 1984, at the Caravilla Retirement Home in Wisconsin.

Don't Rush into Anything so Suddenly! —
Octavio Guillen and Adriana Martinez were married
in June 1969. Both were 82 years old. The couple
had been engaged since 1902! The 67-year
engagement set a world's record.

It Must Be Love - Part 2 — Jack and Edna
Moran of Seattle, Washington, like to prove their
love. The couple has remarried each other 40
times since their first wedding in 1937. Some
places they have been remarried include Banff,
Canada; Cairo, Egypt; and London, England.

The Bride Wore Diapers — The youngest couple to ever marry was an 11-month-old boy and a
3-month-old girl in Bangladesh. The wedding was
arranged to end a 20-year feud between the
couples' families.

Marriage by Moon — The largest mass wedding
ceremony took place when Sun Yung Moon married 6,516 couples in a factory near Seoul, South
Korea, on October 30, 1988. Most of the 13,032
"Moonies" who were married that day had never
met their partner before the ceremony.

Pictured here is Sun Yung Moon, the Reverend who performed the largest mass wedding in history.

A Day to Remember — The most expensive wedding in history took place over seven days in May 1981. The wedding of Mohammed, son of Sheik Rashid Maktoum, to Princess Salama in Dubai cost over $44 million. A stadium that seated 20,000 people was built for the wedding.

She Couldn't Take His Snoring Anymore — The oldest couple to ever get divorced was Ida and Simon Stern of Milwaukee, Wisconsin. He was 97 years old, she was 91 when their marriage was dissolved.

FUN, FOOD AND DRINK

Who Washed All Those Dishes? — The most people ever served at a banquet is 30,000 during a military feast in Radewitz, Poland, on June 15, 1730.

The most people ever served indoors at one time is 18,000 city workers in Paris, France, on August 18, 1889. In modern times, the wedding of two Hasidic Jews on Long Island, New York, attracted between 17,000 and 20,000 people. Meal Mart of Brooklyn provided the kosher catering which included two tons of gefilte fish.

Dinner With a View — A group of mountaineers called the Ansett Social Climbers from Sidney, Australia, put on a formal dinner on top of a 22,205-foot mountain in Peru. The nine climbers scaled the mountain on June 28, 1989, with a dining table, chairs, wine, and a three-course meal. At the summit, they donned top hats, thermal black ties, and ball gowns. Unfortunately, the wine froze.

Bet He Needs to Diet — The world champion at eating out is Fred Magel of Chicago, Illinois, who has dined out 46,000 times in 60 nations. Magel is a restaurant critic.

Parties to Remember — The royal family of Great Britain hosted a children's party to celebrate the "International Year of the Child." The event, held in Hyde Park in London, England, was attended by 160,000 children on May 30 and 31, 1979.

The biggest birthday party ever held was to celebrate the 89 birthday of Colonel Harland Sanders, the founder of Kentucky Fried Chicken. On September 9, 1979, over 35,000 people wished the colonel well in Louisville, Kentucky.

Don't Eat it All — An apple pie measuring 23 feet by 40 feet was baked by chef Glynn Christian in Kent, England. The pie required over 600 bushels of apples and weighed 30,115 pounds.

The largest cherry pie ever made weighed in at 28,355 pounds and measured 17.5 feet across. It was 26 inches deep. The pie contained 25,890 pounds of cherry filling.

They Had to Split — The longest banana split ever made was 4.45 miles long, or 23,496 feet. It was made by the residents of Selinsgrove, Pennsylvania, on April 30, 1988.

That Takes the Cake — The largest cake ever made weighed 128,238 pounds and included 16,209 pounds of icing. It was made to celebrate the 100th birthday of Fort Payne, Alabama.

The tallest cake in the world was over 77 feet high. It was created by 121 people in Indonesia in 1989.

The oldest cake ever found is now on display in a food museum in Switzerland. It was found in the grave of Pepionkh who lived in ancient Egypt about 4,200 years ago. The cake was "vacuum packed" in the tomb and contains sesame, honey, and milk.

Life Savers to the Moon — The top-selling candy in the world are Life Savers. Nearly 35 billion rolls of the candy have been sold since it was introduced in 1913. A tunnel formed by the holes in the middle, placed end to end, would stretch to the moon and back over three times. In 1983, Thomas Syta of Van Nuys, California, made one Life Saver last in his mouth (with the hole intact) for seven hours and ten minutes.

This One Won't Fit in the Microwave — The largest menu item in the world is roasted camel, occasionally prepared for Bedouin wedding feasts.

To prepare the dish, cooked eggs are stuffed into fish, the fish are stuffed into chickens, the chickens are stuffed into roasted sheep, and the sheep are stuffed into a whole camel. Dessert is unnecessary.

Whole Lot of Donut Hole — The largest donut ever made weighed 2,099 pounds and was 22 feet across. It was baked by Ed Sanderson in Crystal River, Florida on December 10, 1988.

A House Good Enough to Eat — A gingerbread house 52 feet tall and 32 feet square was constructed by one 100 people in 1988. The edible house required 2,000 sheets of gingerbread and 1,650 pounds of icing.

Does That Come With Cheese? — The world's largest hamburger, weighing 5,520 pounds, was made at the Outgamie County Fair in Seymore, Wisconsin, on August 5, 1989.

We all Scream for Ice Cream — An ice cream sundae weighing 54,914 pounds was made by Palm Dairies of Edmonton, Canada. The record-breaking treat used 44,689 pounds of ice cream, 9,688 pounds of syrup, and 537 pounds of topping.

Bet That Cost a Lot of Bread — A loaf of bread 2,357 feet 10 inches long was baked by the

Northland Job Corps of Vergennes, Vermont, on November 3, 1987. The almost half-mile-long loaf required 4,480 pounds of charcoal and 4,700 feet of tin foil to bake it.

What a Sucker! — The largest lollipop in the world weighed 2,052 pounds and was made by the Hyatt Regency Memphis Hotel in Tennessee on February 20, 1986.

Shake It Up Baby — A record-breaking 1,891-gallon milk shake was made by Smith Dairy Products in Orrville, Ohio, in 1989.

They Egged Him On — The largest omelet ever cooked was 706 feet across and contained 54,763 eggs and 531 pounds of cheese. It was made in a 30-foot-wide skillet by egg-man Michael McGowen in Las Vegas, Nevada, on October 25, 1986.

And They Didn't Deliver it in 30 Minutes — A pizza measuring 111 feet 3 inches across was baked by Pizza Hut in Singapore on June 9, 1990.

A Chipper Chip — A potato chip 23 inches by 14.5 inches was produced at the Pringles Plant in Jackson, Tennessee. The largest potato chip in the world was made from potato flour.

Ahh Baloney — The longest salami in the world was 61 feet 3.5 inches long and 24 inches across.

The 1,202-pound snack was constructed by Kurtztown Bologna Company in Pennsylvania.

Thirteen Miles of Meat — A sausage 13.125 miles long was made by Keith Boxley in England on June 18, 1988. It took 15 hours, 33 minutes to make the link.

MONUMENTAL MUSICAL MOMENTS

(Musical records are considered valid if the person plays 22 hours a day with a five-minute break each hour.)

The World Accordion to Pieter — The world's record for non-stop accordion playing goes to Pieter van Loggerenberg of South Africa. Van Loggerenberg played his squeeze-box for 85 hours in a row, from July 7 to July 10, 1987.

Multiple Musical Madness — Rory Blackwell holds the record for being the world's largest "one-man band." Blackwell played his "double left-footed perpendicular percussion-pounder, plus his three-tier right-footed horizontal 22-pronged differential beater, and his 12-outlet bellow-powered horn-blower" all at one time. The multiple musical machine consisted of 108 pieces made up of 19 melody and 89 percussion instruments. On May 27, 1985, Blackwell set another record when he played one song on 314 instruments in one minute 23 seconds.

It Was Quite a Pounding — No one in the world has played the drums longer than Trevor Mitchell of Scunthorpe, England. Mitchell pounded the skins for 1,224 hours, or 51 days, from March 20 to May 10, 1990. The American record is held by Don Murphy of Fort Mill, South Carolina, who beat the drums from May 28 to July 18, 1989 — an elapsed time of 1,217 hours or 50 days 17 hours.

After That He Was Too Pooped to Toot — From March 21 to March 23, 1986, Joseph Shury played his flute. This world's record flute tooter played for 61 hours non-stop.

No Second String Players — Vincent Paxton of Winterslow, England, played his guitar for 300 hours from November 23 to December 6, 1986, setting a world's record.

Rick Raven holds the record as the world's fastest guitar player for his solo of 5,400 notes in one minute on April 27, 1989.

All Keyed Up — The record for piano playing is 1,218 hours. To become the piano pounding champion, David Scott of New South Wales, Australia, tickled the keys from May 7 to June 27, 1982, an elapsed time of 51 days, 18 hours.

Rock Around the Clock — The longest time a four-person band has played is 147 hours, or six days, three hours. The Dekorators set the record at Becketts Bar, East Sussex, England, on February 27, 1985.

Swinging Singing Kings — Pastor S. Jeyaseelan of Ramnad, India, sang for 262 hours from March 29 to April 12, 1985, setting the world's solo singing record.

The Apache Junction High School Choir sang 80 hours, one minute in 1989, to set the world's choir singing record.

Wonderful Whistling Winner — Vanka Kumar of India whistled for 45 hours, 20 minutes from May 10 to May 12, 1990.

Yodel-Aye-He-Whooo — No one has ever yodelled longer than Jim Whitman of Tyne, England. Whitman "yodel-aye-he-whooed" for 30 hours, 1 minute in 1989.

SILLY HUMAN TRICKS

An Appealing Peel — The longest, unbroken apple peel on record is 172 feet 4 inches, peeled by Kathy Wafler of Wolcott, New York, on October 16, 1972. The apple-skinning took 11 hours, 30 minutes. The peel weighed 20 ounces.

Sweet Dreams Sharpie — Ken Owens of Pontypridd, Wales, lay on a bed of nails for 300 hours, including over 132 hours without a break. The record- and back-breaking feat lasted for almost 12 days, from May 3 to May 14, 1986.

Sweet Dreams - Part 2 — Nine people from Edinburgh, Scotland, set a world's record by pushing a bed for 3,233 miles, from June 21 to July 26, 1979.

Bicycle Built for 19 — Nineteen members of the Jago Sport Club mounted and rode a single bicycle over 656 feet on June 30, 1988.

Bubble Trouble — A 50-foot-long bubble was created out of dish soap with a bubble wand on June 6, 1988, by David Stein of New York City.

Susan Williams of Fresno, California, holds the world's record for the largest bubble blown with bubble gum. She blew a bubble 22 inches across in June 1985.

Knees to Know You — The longest distance a person has continually crawled on both knees is 28.5 miles. Reg Morris of England accomplished the feat in nine hours, 30 minutes on July 29, 1988. Jagdish Chander of India crawled 870 miles over 15 months, from Aligarh to Jamma, India. He made the journey on his knees to please his favorite Hindu goddess, Mata.

Don't Get These Guys Mad at Your Party — The 15 members of the Black Leopard Karate Club ripped apart a seven-room wooden farmhouse in Alberta, Canada, with their feet and bare hands. The kicking and chopping demolition work took three hours, 18 minutes on June 13, 1982.

Just Skip It — The world's record for stone skipping goes to 69-year-old Arthur Ring who skipped a stone 29 times ("14 plinkers and 15 pitty-pats") at Midway Beach, California, on August 4, 1984.

What Goes Up Must Come Down — No one in the world has ridden an escalator longer than David Beattie and Adrian Simons of London, England. The pair rode the up and down escalators in the Top Shop, a department store, for 101 hours. They each traveled 134 miles.

What a Mess — The world's record for picking up garbage goes to the 64,500 volunteers who cleaned up 2,900 miles of shoreline in the state of Florida on September 23, 1989. The big sweep was part of a clean-up campaign sponsored by the Center for Marine Conservation.

What a Job — Johann Thieme of Aldenburg, Germany, dug 23,311 graves in his 50-year career. That equals over one grave every day for half of a century. In 1826, a co-worker dug Thieme's grave.

What a Lot of Chewing — Between 1969 and 1987, Cathy Ushler of Redmond, Washington, made a gum wrapper chain that was 5,967 feet long. To put that in perspective, one mile equals 5,280 feet.

Hula Hopefuls — Chico Johnson gyrated 81 hula hoops at once on September 9, 1983. Roxanne Rose of Pulman, Washington, gyrated a hula hoop for 90 hours in 1987.

Chico Johnson sets a world record by keeping 100 hula hoops going during the World Hula Hoop contest.

And They All Fell Down — John Sain, 15, of South Bend, Indiana, built a house of cards 12 feet, 10 inches tall. The house of cards had 68 stories.

WHAT NEXT?

This book contains only some of the incredible accomplishments that humans have achieved using their big brains. "Why," you might ask, "would someone need a big brain to push a bed 3,000 miles, or ride a merry-go-round for two weeks?" Maybe if our brains keep growing, we'll be able to figure that out. But human beings are the only animals that know how to laugh and have fun. We invented humor. And it is probably our good sense of humor that has helped us survive these past 100,000 years. That proves that you should have fun and keep smiling. Maybe you could set a world's record!